Analysis of the Cartoons of Raphael

Charles Benjamin Norton

ANALYSIS

OF THE

CARTOONS OF RAPHAEL.

Charles Benjamin Norton, publisher.

———•••———

NEW YORK:

CHARLES B. NORTON,

IRVING BUILDINGS.

1860.

BAKER & GODWIN, PRINTERS,
1 SPRUCE STREET, N. Y.

TO THE SUBSCRIBERS

TO

RAPHAEL'S CARTOONS.

————— •••—————

The undersigned, in presenting this volume to the attention of the reader, would specially express his surprise and gratification at the result of his enterprise. Commenced in December last, he is happy to state that before the ensuing July he had obtained over nine hundred names as subscribers to this set of Plates. As a matter of interest and curiosity, he begs leave to add some statistics relative to the different States, &c., where these Plates have been distributed, to foster, it is believed, a true taste for art and a love for the beautiful. The effect of these engravings in any household cannot but be beneficial ; and it is not too much to expect even a general influence for good upon a whole people, from the distribution of *seven thousand* such works of art.

The subjoined list indicates the State and number of copies distributed.

Maine	10	Georgia	10
New Hampshire	4	Alabama	4
Vermont	73	Mississippi	2
Massachusetts	137	Texas	2
Connecticut	149	Tennessee	3
Rhode Island	20	Kentucky	3
New York	41	Ohio	61
New York City	263	Indiana	16
New Jersey	8	Illinois	14
Pennsylvania	27	Michigan	14
Maryland	14	Wisconsin	9
Virginia	6	Minnesota	1
District of Columbia	3	Iowa	6
North Carolina	11	Missouri	1
South Carolina	10		

Making a grand total of 922 sets—over six thousand separate engravings already distributed.

The subscriber has been advised by the Publishers, Messrs. DAY & SON, of London, that the steel-plates have been destroyed, and therefore these Cartoons become of great value to each possessor. The few remaining sets of the 1000 are now held at $20 the set, at which price they will be disposed of till all are sold.

The ANALYSIS herewith presented, has been prepared with great care by competent parties, from a personal examination of the original paintings in the Gallery at Hampton Court, and it is hoped that it will give satisfaction.

CHARLES B. NORTON,

Agent for Libraries.

CONTENTS.

THE

CARTOONS OF RAPHAEL.

I.

PAUL PREACHING AT ATHENS.

THE eye no sooner glances on this celebrated Cartoon, than it is immediately struck
with the commanding attitude of the speaker,
and the various emotions excited in his hearers.

The interest which the first appearance of
St. Paul at Athens had occasioned, was not
calculated to subside on a sudden; his doctrines were too new, and his zeal too ardent.
From the multitude it ascended to the philoso-

phers. The Epicureans and Stoics particularly
assailed him. Antecedently to the scene described in the picture, among the various
characters already encountered by the Apostle, many, undoubtedly, in their speculations
upon divine subjects, had often imagined a
sublimer religion than that commonly acknow-
ledged: such, therefore, would make it their
business to hear him again. Others, to whom
truth was of less value than the idle amuse-
ment of vain disquisition, felt no other motive
than curiosity. By far the greater part, however, obstinately bigoted to their particular
tenets, and abhorring innovation, regarded
him as impious, or as a mere babbler: these
also wished to hear him again, but with no
other than the insidious view, that by a more
regular and explicit profession of his doctrines
he might expose his own absurdities, or render
himself obnoxious to the State.

With these various motives, and by general
consent, he is brought to the Areopagus, a

place in Athens dedicated to judicial investigation, and frequented by all who were distinguished either for literature or philosophy.

St. Paul, upon this occasion, is not surrounded by a promiscuous and misgoverned throng; everything is conducted with decorum. He is placed on the eminence of Mars-Hill, while his opponents and others arrange themselves around him in silence and expectation. In a moment his mind kindles into that fervor of eloquence which the Athenians so passionately admired; and, while all eyes are directed towards him, he opens his address with the well-known, concise, and dignified exordium—"Ye men of Athens, I perceive that in all things ye are too superstitious; for, as I passed by, and beheld your devotions, I found an altar with this inscription,—To THE UNKNOWN GOD. *Whom, therefore, ye ignorantly worship, him declare I unto you.*"

This seems to be the precise time chosen by the painter; an instant when the animation of

St. Paul was at the highest. His sentiment,
his eyes, his hands, appear to lay hold on
heaven—he stands with more dignified firm-
ness—his whole attitude is full of the sacred
authority of his mission ; and, for the moment
rapt in sublime consciousness, he appears the
minister of a superior Being.

The drapery accords with the majesty of
the figure ; and the light is so managed, especially on the arms and hands, as greatly to
assist the energy of the action.

The conclusion of the period above quoted,
which forms a most impressive pause in the ora-
tion, was not only the best in which to represent the speaker, but no other could have been
chosen so well to characterize the various dis-
positions of his auditors. He charges them
with ignorance and superstition—he engages
to instruct them in a true and sublime theo-
logy—they resent the accusation, and are
incensed at his presumption. No other part
of the whole address was so likely to affect

their feelings, except the mention of the Resurrection; and on that, too much division and
disorder ensued to render it a subject equally
fit for the pencil. All, however, are not supposed to have felt alike; and it is the astonishing display of diversity of mind and variety
of expression which constitutes the first excellence of this picture.

The painter has proceeded, from the warmth
of full conviction, through various gradations,
to the extremes of malignant prejudice and
invincible bigotry.

In the foreground, on the right, is Dionysius, who is recorded to have embraced the
new religion. With the utmost fervor in his
countenance, and with a kind of sympathetic
action and unconscious eagerness, he advances
a step nearer. His eye is fixed on the Apostle—he longs to tell him his conversion, already perhaps preceded by conviction wrought
in his mind by the reasonings of the sacred
teacher on previous occasions in the synagogue,

and in the forum or market-place. He appears not only touched with the doctrines he
receives, but expresses an evident attachment
to his instructor : he would become his host
and protector.

This figure is altogether admirable. The
gracefulness of the drapery and of the hair,
the masculine beauty of the features, the per-
spective drawing of the arms, the life and sentiment of the hands, the right one especially,
are inimitable.

Behind is Demaris, mentioned with him as
a fellow-believer. This is the only female in
the composition ; but the painter has fully
availed himself of the character in assisting his
principle of contrast ; an excellence found in
all the works of Raphael. Her discreet distance, her modest deportment, her pious and
diffident eye, discovering a degree of awe, the
decorum and arrangement of her hair, all interest the mind in her favor.

Next to these, but at some distance, is a

Stoic. The first survey of this figure conveys the nature of his peculiar philosophy, dignity, and austerity. Raphael has well understood what he meant in this instance to illustrate. His head is sunk on his breast; his arms are mechanically folded; his eyes, almost shut, glance towards the ground; he is absorbed in reflection. In spite of his stoicism, discomposure and perplexity invade his soul, mixed with a degree of haughty mortification.

Sir Joshua Reynolds has observed, that " the same idea is continued through the whole figure, even to the drapery, which is so closely muffled about him, that even his hands are not seen;" and that " by this happy correspondence between the expression of the countenance and the disposition of the parts, the figure appears to think from head to foot."

Behind the Stoic are two young men, well contrasted in expression; anger in the elder, and in the other, youthful pride half abashed, are finely discriminated.

Beyond, in the same continued half-circle with the Stoic, is perhaps exhibited the most astonishing contrast ever imagined—that of inexorable sternness and complete placidity.— Of the two figures, the first is denominated a Cynic, who, disappointed in his expectation of the ridiculous appearance which he conceived the Apostle, when confronted, would make among them, abandons his mind to rage. His formidable forehead concentrates its whole expression; with a fixed frown, and threatening eye, he surveys the object of his indignation. He alone would engage to confute him, or punish his temerity. His eager impatience and irritation are not discovered in his features only; he raises his heel from the ground, and leans with a firmer pressure on his crutch, which seems to bend beneath him.

Pass from him to the more polished Epicurean. This figure exhibits perfect repose of body and mind: no passions .agitate the one, no action discomposes the other. His hands,

judiciously concealed beneath beautiful drapery, show there can be no possible motion or
employment for them. His feet seem to sleep
upon the ground. His countenance, which is
highly pleasing, and full of natural gentleness,
expresses only a smile of pity at the fancied
errors of the Apostle, mingled with delight
derived from his eloquence. He waits with
an inclined head in passive and serene expectation. If a shrewd intelligence is discovered in
his eyes, it is too gentle to disturb the general
expression of tranquility.

Behind are two other young men: the first
discovers a degree of superciliousness with his
vexation; his companion is more disgusted and
more morose.

These, and the two young figures previously
described, are not introduced merely to fill up
the group: they may be intended as pupils to
the philosophers before them, though by some
considered as young Romans, who have introduced themselves from ennui or curiosity.

1*

Beyond is a character in whose mind the force of truth and eloquence appears to have produced conviction; but pride, vanity, or self-interest, impel him to dissemble. His finger placed upon the upper lip, shows that he has imposed silence upon himself.

In the center is seated a group from the Academy. The skill of Raphael in this instance is eminent. These figures are not only thrown into shade, to prevent their interference with the principal figure, but, from their posture, they contribute to its elevation, and at the same time vary the line of the standing group.

It seems as if the old philosopher in profile on the left, had offered some observations on the Apostle's address, and that he was eagerly listening to the reply of his sage friend, in whose features we behold more of the spirit of mild philosophy. The action of his fingers denotes his habit of reasoning, and regularity of argument. The middle figure behind appears to be watching the effect which his remarks would produce.

The action of the young man pointing to the Apostle characterizes the keen susceptibility and impetuosity of his age. His countenance expresses disgust approaching to horror. The other young man turns his head round, as though complaining of unseasonable interruption. The drapery of both the front figures in this group is finely drawn: the opening action of the knees in the one is beautifully followed and described by the folds; in the other, the compression, in consequence of the bent attitude, is equally executed; the turn of the head gives grace and variety to the figure.

The head introduced beyond, and rather apart, is intended to break the two answering lines of the dark contour of the Apostle's drapery, and the building in the back-ground.

In the group placed behind the Apostle the mind is astonished at the new character of composition. The finest light imaginable is thrown upon the sitting figure, and as necessary a mass of shade is cast upon the two others.　•

It is difficult to ascertain what or whom Raphael meant by that corpulent and haughty personage wearing the cap. His expression, however, is evident. Malice and vexation are depicted in his countenance. His stride, and the action of his hand, are characteristic of his temperament.

The figure standing behind is supposed to be a Magician. His dark hair and beard, which seem to have been neglected, and the "keen mysterious gaze" of his eye, certainly exhibit a mind addicted to unusual studies.

Under him, the only remaining figure is one who listens with malignant attention, as though intending to report everything. He has the aspect of a spy. His eye is full of danger to the Apostle; and he crouches below, that he may not be disturbed by communication.

If this figure be considered with reference to Dionysius, it may be remarked that Ra-phael has not only contrasted his characters, but even the two ends of his picture. By this means the greatest possible force is given to the subject. At the first survey, the subordinate contrasts may escape the eye ; but these greater oppositions must have their effect.

When from this detailed display of the Cartoon, the eye again glances over the whole subject, including the dignity of the architecture; the propriety of the statue of Mars, which faces his temple ; the happy management of the landscape, with the two conversation figures ; the result must be, an acknowledgment that in this one effort of art is combined all that is great in drawing, in expression, and in composition.

II.

PASCE OVES MEAS.   FEED MY SHEEP.

THE CHARGE TO PETER.

THAT power of discriminating character which is so admirably displayed in the Cartoon of ST. PAUL AT ATHENS, has been exerted with equal success on the present subject.

. The difficulty attending the execution of the former was, perhaps, in some degree lessened by the necessary introduction of the Philosophers, whose different opinions would naturally suggest to the mind of Raphael not only variety of countenance, but those peculiar traits which were calculated to distinguish one sect from another.

The painter had not the advantage of any such incidental assistance in the subject of THE CHARGE TO PETER. The body of Disciples, brought together in one group, could not with propriety exhibit that studied contrast of character which marked the Epicurean and the Cynic ; they could only display that diversity which a number of men, selected from various classes, influenced by different temperaments, and possessing unequal degrees of dignity and intelligence, might naturally be expected to discover.

The three characters, however, of Peter, James, and John, which are so distinctly portrayed by the Evangelists, afforded the most favorable opportunity Raphael himself could wish, to display that individuality of expression and gesture, by which each of these Disciples is at once distinguished.

In the development of this Cartoon, it is not easy to point out which of its properties first claims the attention. The interest and emotion which animate the group are so immediately communicated to the spectator, that it may obtain the general denomination of a picture of sympathy. And perhaps the first detached excellences which excite admiration, are the prevailing dignity of the figures, and the judicious space which is interposed between the Disciples and the exalted object before them.

This last circumstance, which cannot escape the feeling observer, not only communicates additional majesty to the Master, but indicates in the greatest degree the governing sentiment of his followers, upon this interesting interview.

Instead of familiarly crowding around him, which would have implied an insensibility to the striking event of his appearance to them after his Resurrection, they seem, by their

distance, to be conscious of the new relation
in which they stand. Their attention is
nevertheless strongly excited to that solemn
communication which Christ particularly addressed to Peter, and of which the rest were
the interested witnesses and hearers.

The scene of the picture is at the Sea of
Tiberias, on which some of the Disciples had
been employed in their avocation of fishing.
But, in order to put the reader in full posses-
sion of the subject, it is necessary to advert
to that part of the preceding narration with
which it is connected.

At the last solemn meeting which Christ
held with his disciples before his death, he
foretold that in his sufferings they would all
desert him; but Peter, at that time sincere in
the expression of his zeal, exclaimed with
great animation, that he at least would not be
of that number. Christ's prediction, however,
that this Apostle would deny him, was fully
verified. And, perhaps, it was in allusion to

his threefold denial, that upon the present occasion the Saviour pathetically addressed him three times in the following words: " Lovest thou me more than these ? " adding, after the several answers of Peter, "Feed my sheep."

The point of time chosen by the painter, is that of the *first* question and subsequent charge; because this period afforded an opportunity of describing a stronger expression among the Disciples, as it was the first moment of their arrested attention, and consequent surprise. Upon the *second* reiteration, Peter would have discovered more emotion, and John could not have been in the act of advancing. The time of the *third* cannot be supposed, because Peter's grief was then great; and it is likely the other disciples would have drawn nearer the Saviour, in order to present themselves to him, and partake his notice. And their surprise must at that time have been changed into assurances of zeal and attachment.

In analyzing the individual characters of
which this Cartoon is composed, the first that
engages the mind is the sublime figure of
Christ; which conveys, to the utmost possible extent, the idea of a superior being risen
from the dead ! The body partially covered,
the continued sympathetic action of the hands,
and the half-averted majesty of the attitude,
equally promote the painter's intention.

When the head is contemplated, we cannot
help feeling that Raphael has discovered pow-
ers surpassing all his other efforts, in proportion as his task was more difficult.

To portray the mind, the manners, and the
passions of men, was his great province and
peculiar talent. In this instance he had to
give form and feature to Divinity; with human lineaments to develop what is never seen
in man,—expression without passion, a face
perfectly free from the traces of moral frailty.

Addison has remarked a trait of recent suffering in the countenance. This was necessary
in order to blend with the dignity of Christ,

that sympathy which was indicative of the affinity of his nature to man; and to recall to the mind those tragical events which preceded the Resurrection.

The eyes are a little elevated above Peter, to allow that Disciple an opportunity the more steadfastly to regard his divine Master, and to imply also a degree of solemn abstraction.

The mouth, a little opened, shows that Peter has rejoined, and that Christ is about to repeat his address.*

The drapery thrown over the body is beautiful and consistent: it forms one entire garment, and is finely folded.

The head and figure of Peter are perfectly characteristic of his simplicity; without appearing to comprehend the full extent of the question put to him, but subdued by the personality of the address, he has fallen on the

---

* The head of Christ in the original is a little injured by damp, but it was not difficult to discover the lines. The expression is not at all damaged.

ground, and appears to have made his answer
with his usual sincerity of manner, but with
less fervor and confidence. What was want-
ing in words he supplies by his attitude, full
of tenderness, humility, and reverence. The
more entirely to establish the propriety of the
supplicatory posture, it must be considered,
that Peter was perfectly conscious of the allusion of Christ's address to that part of his conduct already referred to. This figure, in its
effect, is finely poised by the advanced position
of the right knee, and by the piece of drapery
extending on the ground around it.

Behind Peter, John is seen advancing to the
front, with a countenance the most benign and
affectionate. He seems as if he was about to
assure his Lord that his love was at least equal
to Peter's; for whom, however, the sympathy
so exquisitely blended in his expression, indicates much compassion, and perhaps an intention to intercede.

Affection for his Master, and kindness for

his friend and fellow-disciple, pervade the whole figure. The uplifted hands are pressed together, as preparatory to the utterance of some interesting sentiment; and his ardor is beautifully expressed by the impulse which naturally carries him nearer the object of his regard.

In the original, there is a beautiful suffusion of deep red on the cheek, indicative of the soft vivacity and ardent affection, which were predominant in the breast of the Apostle John.

Before John is James: the expression of whose countenance it is not easy to explain. While it seems descriptive of awe and reverence, it also indicates a degree of dissatisfaction. This trait, however, rather approaches the expression of gravity than that of anger, and may be intended not only to characterize this Apostle, but to denote surprise at the affectionate manner in which Peter's crime was noticed by his Lord. These three Disciples are distinguished from the other Apostles in

all the Cartoons in which they appear: they
were the individuals whom Christ generally
selected to attend him upon the most interesting occasions. But it will not, perhaps, be un-
acceptable to the subscriber, to pursue the
analysis through the rest of the Disciples,
whom it would be difficult to name, although
it is highly probable Raphael characterized
each in his own mind.

The head, behind John, seen almost in front,
is full of simplicity and goodness. The eyes,
full of devotion, are modestly and reveren-
tially directed towards Christ. Possibly, from
the expression and situation of this figure, Raphael might have designed it for Andrew,
Simon Peter's brother.

The eagerness of the neighboring profile is a
fine contrast to the head of John. The figure
seems equally anxious with that Apostle, to
express his love to his Master; but without
that delicacy and softness by which the bosom
friend of the Redeemer was distinguished.

His ardor is plainly mingled with anxiety and impatience.

The front head next in succession, displays the most powerful emotion, and well comports with the lofty majesty of the figure. His attitude, and the expression of his countenance, discover astonishment at Christ's condescension to Peter; and by the force of his look, he seems to endeavor to communicate his meaning to the Disciple nearest him. The action of the head is an admirable contrast to the general direction of the rest. His hand, however, connects him with the revered object of their common attention, and helps to preserve the beautiful unity of the design.

The elegant figure addressed by the person last described, represents a very different character. His candid countenance is full of uninquiring acquiescence, mixed with agreeable surprise.

The whole design of this figure is graceful, and is another instance by which Raphael dis-

2

covers his pre-eminence over other masters, in the conformity he invariably introduces between the superior and subordinate parts. One hand delicately raised to press the inner drapery to the bosom, leaves the other in the act of gently folding round him the extending mantle, which gracefully flows over his shoulder to the ground. This action, and the gentle bend of one knee, bear an equally significant correspondence with the serenity of the head.

The Disciple behind endeavors to look through the group, without making himself conspicuous. The Abbé du Bos, misled by the prying cast of the countenance, pronounced this figure to be Judas Iscariot: a strange mistake for an ecclesiastic, who forgot that only eleven Disciples were introduced, and that Judas committed suicide before the Resurrection.*

* The number of Disciples actually present upon this occasion was only seven. Raphael no doubt was aware of this, but probably thought he might be allowed to suppose the whole body present. A painter has his license as well as the poet; and who that contemplates this Cartoon would wish the number reduced to seven?

Neither does the face convey the idea of the baseness and avarice which doubtless were stamped on the features of the traitor. It rather expresses the dejected spirit of deep study; an expression which the book held under the drapery strongly enforces.

The two heads behind are completely apostolic. The one whose eyes are piously raised is full of dignity, sweetness, and intelligence; and seems to intimate a mind connecting with the present scene, the past events that bore relation to it.

The other, equally dignified, is more commanding, and his half-opened mouth indicates that he listens with great attention to the dialogue passing between Christ and Peter.

The last figure has been supposed to be intended for Thomas, whose incredulity the painter intended to describe by the averted position of the head, and the remoteness of his situation. The piece of drapery under the arm finely bears the contour of the figure, and

the general form of the group; and connects
it with the boat, which would otherwise have
produced an unpleasant effect on the eye, by
forming too great a contrast of lines.

The keys held by Peter have nothing to do
with the present subject. They were figura-
tively presented by Christ on a much earlier
occasion. He is therefore generally invested
with them by most painters; but from their
introduction in this Cartoon, it has often, by a
strange misconception, borne the title of "The
Delivery of the Keys."

The introduction of the sheep has, by some,
been censured as too local, or literal; but Raphael remembered that Christ was in the common practice of referring to different objects
around him, in order to illustrate his commu-
nications; and that it might be very fairly
supposed, on such an occasion, a flock of sheep
were feeding near nim. On this account he is
to be justified, as well as in their emblematical
signification. They are of importance, also,

not only as an illustration of the subject, but as connected in effect with the drapery of the principal figure; to the shadowy side of which they form a finer and more diversified relief than the ground could have done.

The whole landscape is pastoral and picturesque; and the elevated horizon contributes not only to embody the effect of the figures, by affording a fine rich contrast to the lights and gentle tones, but in harmonizing and supporting the deep shadows. To an attentive observer, the propriety and fitness of every object in the landscape will also be manifest. The water introduced is part of the Sea of Tiberias, already mentioned as the scene of the picture.

Such is the general analysis of this admirable Cartoon; but to know how closely the painter has attended to the main design of the Evangelical History, it is necessary to refer to the connected narration, which is to be found in the last chapter of St. John's Gospel.

III.

THE DEATH OF ANANIAS.

Audiens Ananias hæc verba Cecidit et expiravit

———————

IT is difficult to survey this Picture without being powerfully impressed by the prevailing dignity of its composition. The grandeur of the design, heightened on the one hand by the astonishment and terror, and on the other softened by the pity and commiseration of the spectators grouped around the victim of supernatural punishment, affects the mind with an interest that belongs both to the truth of history, and the force of the tragic drama.

The eye, glancing around this magnificent circle of figures, at once perceives the various characters of judge, criminal, and witnesses, described by the different expressions of indignation and authority, conviction and death, fear and grief.

The beautiful episode on the left, of the benevolent John, dispensing gifts with all the grace, tenderness, and warmth of charity, is essentially connected with the story of the catastrophe represented.

The converts of the Apostles surrendered all their property for distribution to the poor. Ananias, only assuming that virtue, retained clandestinely the greater part of his; and it was this crime of deliberate hypocrisy, and the solemn falsehood with which he accompanied his partial offering, that brought down upon him the infliction of that sudden and terrible death exhibited by Raphael.

So perfect is the execution of this Cartoon, that the difficulty which the Painter had to encounter, and the consummate art by which he surmounted it, are not at first discovered; but on examination, we soon perceive the ad-

dress with which the groups in the foreground
are so disposed, as both to support the principal figure of Ananias, and to display without
interposition of object, the majestic body of
the Apostles, who, at a dignified distance from
their followers, stand associated in their severe
and holy function.

In the midst of these, St. Peter, who pronounced the fatal sentence, is eminently conspicuous. His countenance exhibits a terrible
self-possession, excited by the certainty that
his denunciation would instantly be accomplished.

Such was the nature of the crime, that his
justice is altogether unattempered by mercy;
not only the expression of his face, but the action of his arm and hand, his firm attitude,
and whole deportment, show him to be the
inflexible judge, in whom there is neither the
hesitation of doubt, nor the thought of
pardon.

His coadjutors experience various emotions,

2*

and display in different degrees the appearances of piety, concern, and holy indignation.
One, on the right of Peter, appeals to Heaven
with the sublimest expression of reverential
awe ; his upraised eyes, and hands fervently
pressed together, exhibit a look and attitude
of the most perfect devotion : such an expression is a fine comment on the atrocity of the
crime committed, and materially supports the
serious interest of the Picture. A prominent
figure on the opposite side directs his regard
to the people, whose attention he endeavors
to fix upon that superior Power without whose
superintendence the impious fraud and falsehood would not have been discovered, nor its
detection followed by so sudden and exem-
plary a punishment. The figure on the left of
Peter surveys the prostrate criminal with an
amiable and elevated compassion. One general sentiment, however, of participation in the
authority of the immediate organ of the divine
interposition connects the whole, and diffuses

over this solemn array of apostolic fellowship
an appearance of indescribable sacredness of
character.

The figure of Ananias, prone and convulsed
in the foreground, produces an effect on those
about him admirably contrasted to the awful
and judicial stillness of the Apostles. Partially clothed, in order more effectually to distinguish him, he exhibits death struggling in
his limbs and muscles, as well as laboring in
his countenance: he is agitated by that last
effort of nature, which, in a moment, will
leave him extended on the marble floor a lifeless corpse. The character of the face is finely
conceived; and it may here be observed, that
Raphael never gives to his guilty or vulgar
personages heroic features—a fault often seen
in other Painters. With regard also to the
scanty drapery about the figure, perhaps it
may not altogether be a conceit to imagine,
that Ananias, in order to confirm the decep-
tion of his pretended surrender of his whole

property, might have divested himself even of
the superfluous part of his daily raiment. To
those who are best acquainted with Raphael,
his skill in human nature, and the address with
which he avails himself of every circumstance
that can illustrate his subject, cannot be exag-
gerated.

The figures next in importance after Ananias and the Apostles, are those immediately
in front of the dying object: and it is in consequence of this situation, that the effect of
terror is more forcibly displayed in them than
in the groups behind Ananias, to whom the
dreadful transition from life to death was not
so instantaneously apparent.

Horror and amazement are indeed blended
to their utmost possible extent of expression
in the character of the man possibly intended
for Joses, who is mentioned to have contri-
buted his possessions a short time before.
Struck with consternation, he has fallen on his
knee, and for an instant seems fixed to the

ground. The whole design of this superior personage is, in the opinion of those best qualified to decide, in the highest degree perfect, and would form a model for the sculptor equal to any of the remains of Greece.

The female behind him discovers her alarm in a manner in every respect suited to her sex; her fear compels her to turn round, as if preparing for flight. Her expressive countenance, notwithstanding its agitation, retains its natural beauty, and finely harmonizes with the elegance of her form. The tastefulness of her hair, partly braided and in part bound with a fillet, indicates a natural gracefulness, softness of manners, and dignity of station, unaccustomed to exhibitions of depravity and scenes of terror.

The two figures at the head of Ananias are strikingly varied: the one wearing a turban, manifests a mixed emotion of curiosity and fear; his timidity is discovered by the retraction of his body, and of that knee next the

object of his contemplation. He is determined, however, to wait the issue of the event.
In this figure there is more surprise than pain,
more disposition to shun contamination than
assist distress. The character is complete, and
shows great originality of invention.

The younger one, pointing upward, bears
the expression of painful solicitude for the
state of the dying man: his manner seems to
denote an interest beyond that of a simple
spectator; and it may be conjectured, from
the general appearance of the figure, as well
as from the style of the drapery, which resembles that of the Apostles, that Raphael
intended this personage for Matthias, the disciple, who had previously been chosen to complete the number of the twelve, after the
defection of Judas. In harmony with this
supposition, his place as conductor of the people upon this occasion of general benevolence,
is well imagined.

The female advancing at the extremity of

the Picture, appears entirely absorbed by her own concerns : and although the most natural and simple idea seems to be, that Raphael has on one side of his Picture placed the rich, bringing their contributions (without reference to any particular character), and, on the other, the poor receiving relief;. yet, the scrupulosity with which she counts her money, and the vexation depicted in her countenance, produced by the intended and apparently reluctant sacrifice of property, have led some to suppose that Raphael intended her for Sapphira: but, admitting this to have been his design, it was not because he was ignorant that she made her appearance before the Apostles a considerable time after her husband's death, but that he might enforce his subject by recalling to the mind the affecting sequel of the story, of which he could not have formed another composition without monotony or inconsistent novelty.

The young men with linen, one of whom

discovers an interesting sympathy, may either
be supposed to be bringing garments for the
general stock, or conceived to be the attendants who are said to have arisen, bound the
body, and carried it out. As the whole was
a short scene, this license of the Painter may
be allowed, in order that the entire history
might be presented. Perhaps Raphael intended to call to the mind the Jewish custom
of immediate concealment of death.

The groups on the left of the Picture, detached from the catastrophe, and for the moment entirely occupied by their own wants
and affairs, display the beautiful scene of the
communion of Poverty and Benevolence: the
distance of their situation, although not great,
is skillfully assisted by the contrivance adopted
by Raphael of showing the back of the head
only of the nearest supplicant.

The mind, turning from the spectacle of
horror in front, reposes awhile upon this exhibition of charity and gratitude, patient

expectation, and humble and importunate petition; and after surveying the zealous readiness of James, who holds the alms-money, and the angelic softness of John, whose gentle features and flowing hair discover a heart quite in unison with one hand that gives, and the other which blesses, returns to behold the tragic part of the composition with double effect.

To some readers it may not perhaps be superfluous to observe, that the manner of ecclesiastical benediction in the church of Rome, is precisely as represented in the Apostle John, by the elevation of two fingers.

It is difficult in this place to suppress an allusion to the amiable Raphael, who so appositely selected this Apostle to shed interest over this subordinate part of his Picture.

The general harmony of the design is preserved by the decrepid old man attended by a female ascending the distant steps ; and part of a figure, placed at an opening in the building, carries the attention gradually away.

The draperies in the Cartoon are universally fine. The flowing and graceful garments of the Apostles, the shorter and handsome dresses of those who may be supposed to have different avocations, the varied garb of aged poverty and youthful destitution, as seen in the old man and kneeling orphans, the apparently foreign attire of the sick mother and daughter, mark the distinction of the numerous characters, and give, not variety only, but reality, to the scene.

In the disposition of the lights and shades, (regarded separately from the general effect) it will be observed that the masses in and about the foreground figures are scattered agreeably to the agitation of the scene; while in the other parts of the Picture they aid the majesty, the softness, and the repose, of the different groups.

When these secondary excellences are reviewed in connection with the more essential beauties of expression of countenance, truth of attitude, and propriety of situation, the majority will doubtless pronounce this Painting the finest effort of the Art.

IV.

ELYMAS THE SORCERER STRUCK WITH BLINDNESS.

" Et confestim cecidit in eum caligo et tenebræ." Acts xiii. 11.

———————

THE Apostles Paul and Barnabas, having promulgated with considerable success the doctrines of Christianity through a great part of the island of Cyprus, were invited by Sergius Paulus, Proconsul of Asia, then residing at Paphos, to discuss the subject in his presence. The importance which the Proconsul attached to the interview may be estimated by the terms in which he addressed his message: "he desired to hear the word of God."

It is probable that he was not governed

only on this occasion by the wish to satisfy his
own judgment, but that he also considered it
his duty in his magisterial capacity to know
something of so striking an innovation on
received opinions.   •

Some popular effervescence might have been
manifested : for it cannot be imagined that the
Apostle, who had opposed himself to the refined, but erring, disputations of the Athenian
philosophers, sparing neither the Platonist, the
Stoic, nor the Epicurean, would hesitate to
refute with his accustomed energy the soph-
isms, and rebuke with the warmth of fervent
zeal the depraved habits of the votaries of the
Paphian Venus.

The audience of the Apostles, therefore, being public, Raphael has chosen the judgment-
seat of the Roman deputy for the scene of his
picture.

It was doubtless in this situation that St.
Paul, obeying the order of the Proconsul, encountered the malignant antagonist who forms

the third personage in this dramatic composition.

This man, being a Jew, adopted amongst his countrymen, for the promotion of his sinister purposes, the character of a prophet; but practiced, in his association with the Greeks, the arts of a magician; and was, therefore, called by them, Elymas the Sorcerer.

Vain of the influence which he possessed in the household of the Proconsul, and fearing the overthrow of an occupation that could only receive encouragement in the center of depraved morals and superstitious ignorance, this shameless individual dared to confront the Apostle, even during his address in the Roman court, and either by injurious accusations, or artful contradictions, attempted to excite the prejudices of the Proconsul.

Thus interrupted, St. Paul, conscious of the power with which he was invested for the punishment of irreclaimable vice, as well as for the dissemination of truth, suddenly drop-

ping the argument, fixed his eyes on the intruder, and said, " O, full of all subtlety and
all mischief! thou child of the devil, thou en-
emy of all righteousness, wilt thou not cease
to pervert the right ways of the Lord? and
now, behold, the hand of the Lord is upon
thee, and thou shalt be blind, not seeing the
sun for a season." The effect was instantane-
ous : "immediately there fell on him a mist and
a darkness, and he went about seeking some
to lead him by the hand."

The solemnity of a public hearing is well
represented in this picture by the disposition
of the figures, the style of the building, and
the general arrangement of subordinate parts.

St. Paul, on the left, stands in the attitude
of denunciation : his figure is noble and commanding ; his expression energetic and formidable: from the words used by him in his
address to Elymas, may be understood the
sublime nature of the subject on which he had
been expatiating, and which required all the

skill of the painter to indicate in the appearance and demeanor of the Apostle.

The drapery which invests him is magnificent; the light proceeds along his arm, and,
terminating at his pointing finger, carries with
it the force of an electric discharge.

How well contrasted is this chief of the
Apostles, to the miserable, the depraved, and
dejected object before him! Fallen in a moment from the height of defiance and insolence
of contradiction, the foiled magician exhibits
blindness and darkness in every part of him.
The preternatural mist seems to hide him from
himself: his eyes irresistibly sealed, he discovers by his open mouth, contracted brows, and
dilated nostrils, the horror which pervades
him. Enveloped in sudden darkness, he in-
stinctively throws out his arms and hands, and
by the projection of his right leg assists his
tottering balance. The figure seems at once
to shrink from danger, and to feel for support
in the meditated retreat for which he is pre-
3

paring; the action of the right hand is particularly adapted to his situation. Throughout the whole design, what higher expression
could be given, to describe the effect of a sudden obscuration of surrounding objects, succeeded by the dreary vacuity, which, in the
midst of numbers, involved friends, enemies,
and place, in indistinguishable night?

The very dress of this character is descriptive; the drapery or cap which enfolds his
head, seems well suited for the occasional en-
velopment of his features, when engaged in
the practice of his vile impostures. In tracing
the figure downwards, the propriety of the
position of the feet cannot be left unnoticed:
it will be observed that they are insensibly
and naturally drawn inward to avoid obsta-
cles.

The Proconsul, elevated in the center, discovers surprise and indignation: seated with
great dignity as judge and arbiter, he yet
shows how deeply his mind had been affected

by the discourse of the Apostle : the side which he had taken is evident in the disgust which his regard of the sorcerer evinces, towards whom he seems involuntarily to have changed his position. There is in his features a judicial acquiescence in the propriety of the punishment. Contempt and resentment must have been produced by the insult offered to him and the Apostle, whose attendance was the result of an express mandate. But for the dignity of his office, it is plain he would rise from his seat : so sudden and alarming, however, was the exhibition of Divine power, that he cannot refrain from extending his arms with something of an action simultaneous with that of the object he surveys.

This figure, whether in feature or dress, is entirely Roman. Not a part is neglected : from the wreath of bay on the head to the elegant sandals that adorn the feet, all is appropriate.

The general effect of this apostolic judgment on the spectators is correctly exhibited.

The rough figure, looking with a scrutinizing glance in the magician's face, as if to
satisfy himself of the fact, cannot conceal his
amazement, which approaches to horror: his
uplifted hands not only show his emotion, but
seem intended, especially the left, to protect
him from the chance of sudden collision with
the sightless impostor, now unconscious of his
direction.

The female behind Elymas is supposed by
some to be intended to represent his wife.
Alarmed by the denunciation of the Apostle,
and confirmed in her fear of its accomplishment by the expression and explanatory action of the figure at the side of the picture, she
seems advancing with impetuous clamor, ex-
hibiting in her manner the utmost vexation
and resentment at the author of her husband's
calamity: she points with a degree of detesta-
tion at the Apostle, scarcely inclined to credit
the extent of his power, but for the assurance
of the individual on whom she directs her expressive look.

The group behind seem to participate in the feelings of this female, without knowing the precise cause. The old man nearest her, who has the aspect of a priest, relies upon the information conveyed by the action of the figure before alluded to, whose quick and animated motions are peculiarly descriptive. His shrewd face betrays, however, more interest at the result of the contest, than anxiety about the cause. This figure absolutely speaks, and is altogether beautifully designed : his erect attitude is a good contrast to the discomfited and bending magician.

The sedate, yet stern, face of the old man beyond is extremely interesting ; he regards the Apostle as doubtful of the propriety of his doctrines, and seems to question the nature of the judicial authority exercised by him. His gravity belongs as much to the scene of which he is a witness, as to his advanced age. The fine light thrown on this old man's head produces great effect, and confers a striking individuality of character.

The life of this part of the picture is strongly supported by the curious and importunate physiognomy of the corpulent man in the background; he seems anxious to know what is going forward, and presses himself between his neighbors, endeavoring to catch the rumor of the scene.

The personage on the left of the Proconsul appears to be a friend or attendant in some superior official capacity: with a delicate and refined air he turns his head toward the figure behind him, and expresses by his action, which is unaffectedly dignified, his sentiments on the occasion: he appears to take the opportunity of representing the consequence of opposing truth with a malignant spirit: the individual to whom he addresses himself shows by his action and look the effect produced on his mind.

The bearers of the fasces on the right of the Proconsul, and the figures beyond, keep up the animation of the subject by different gestures and expressions. The Lictor most in shade,

betrays an appearance of youthful commisser-
ation, which is also evinced in the coarser features of his companion on the upper step.

The sublime and pious countenance of Barnabas, who is placed on the left of St. Paul,
reminds the spectator of the Divine nature of
the apostolic mission, which for a moment had
been diverted from its original object. He
casts his eyes upward, and indicates, by his
devout regard and uplifted hand, the source
and dependence of that miraculous power,
which was not only imparted to punish wick-
edness, but to confirm the truth of the Christian doctrine in the conversion of the Proconsul.

The light and shade through this picture is
distributed with great truth and force: the
back-ground, which relieves the figure of the
principal Apostle, brings him forward in the
most prominent manner, and, in combination
with the majesty of the design, renders him
the most important object in the composition.

Elymas is partly obscured by a dark drapery : the lights which distinguish the head,
arms, and legs of the figure, make him, however, sufficiently conspicuous, without destroy-
ing that indistinctness which seems necessary
to convey a feeling of the sudden darkness
which enveloped him : this effect is heightened
by the contrast of the sunny lights which, in-
tersected by dark shadows, play upon the elegant pavement.

There is a truth in this work of art that
renders the spectator immediately acquainted
with the subject.

The distinction of character in the Apostles,
the magistrate, and the magician, accords exactly with the conceptions that are naturally
felt upon the first comprehension of the story.

The figures are neither too few nor too numerous : the dignity of the occasion would be
disturbed by a confused group pressing together in the foreground—an impropriety
which could not be atoned for by any variety

of attitude and expression. The scene is not intended to represent the trial of an individual, but a solemn audience for the explanation of important doctrines : the actors being few, no skill could convey a higher appearance of impassioned feeling, consistent with the decorum of consular superintendence.

The open space in front diffuses dignity and air through the picture, and is necessary to show the superior figure of the Proconsul, for whose satisfaction and conviction the Apostles were summoned.

A subject so beautifully treated, endears the mind to an art which renders permanent evanescent expression of countenance, and exhibits a lasting reference for the forms of dignity and the modes of passion.

V.

THE

MIRACULOUS DRAUGHT OF FISHES.

Noli timere : ex hoc jam homines eris capiens.—LUKE v. 10.

Upon a comparison of this subject with the
other Cartoons, a superficial observer might
imagine that Raphael had too limited a number of figures before him to enable him to fill
the mind with that interest, and excite those
emotions, which a pencil like his ought to
command, and which in the other composi-
tions in this series of paintings he had shown
himself so capable of producing.

Such is the power of nature, that when
skillfully and faithfully exhibited, she is
equally mistress of the feelings, whether she

presents herself in her greatest variety of human passion, or shows only a single example of occasional sentiment and momentary expression.

Perfection like this is more demonstrated by the absence of the ornaments of art, than assisted by them; and triumphs by commanding those original principles of sympathy, which are inseparably connected with our being.

But there are harmonies in nature which an inventive mind will discover, the introduction of which will essentially promote the intended effect by exciting the imagination and calling into action corresponding and relative ideas.

In this picture a majestic solitude contributes, by the contrast of its tranquillity, to heighten the intensity of human feeling, and exalt the sacredness of Divinity. An elevated horizon limits the waters of a capacious lake, diffused with the sublimity of the ocean, and bounded in the foreground by a lonely and unfrequented shore, whose desertion is marked by scattered shells, and the presence of a few water-birds preying for fish. The interesting groups of men, and women with their children, that animate the distant architectural landscape, show that something unusual has preceded the present scene; and indicate also that what is occurring was not an isolated circumstance, beginning and ending with itself, but connected with the general benefit of the people; for Peter, after this miracle, became an Apostle of Christ, and teacher of his brethren.

From the history it appears that Christ, after having instructed the multitude from a vessel in which he had entered in order to avoid the pressure of the throng, desired Peter and his companions to leave the shore and recede into deep water for the purpose of fishing.

It is necessary, in order to comprehend

the full meaning of the scene exhibited, to remind the reader that Peter and the rest had been out to catch fish the preceding night, without success, and therefore urged with Christ the inutility of repeating the attempt, thinking that the time was either not seasonable or not propitious: they had no expectation that upon so ordinary an occasion their master would exercise a power which ultimately helped to confirm his mission, and made Peter and the rest his devoted followers.

The mandate however was obeyed, and the nets cast into the water; in a moment they were filled to repletion, and the boats in apparent danger of sinking.

Is it possible to survey the figure of Christ without acknowledging an appearance very different from the display of mere human power? The superiority is equally shown in the act and in the manner; a placid dignity of mien, a parental regard, a soothing action, an undisturbed attitude, are all combined in a figure intended to show the master of nature and the friend of man. He perceives the agitated state of Peter, and with the mildest accents addresses him thus: "Fear not; from henceforth thou shalt catch men." A phrase easily understood by one accustomed to the avocation of the net. One can almost imagine these words proceeding from those gentle lips, which seem only capable of compassionate and benign expression.

Can it excite surprise that upon such an event Peter should yield to the mingled emotions of fear, respect, supplication, humility, and veneration? The language which he uttered, "Depart from me, for I am a sinful man, O Lord," was an expression that is perfectly embodied in the picture; and it is difficult to say whether the words or the features of the humble fisherman are the best interpreters of his heart. It seems as if all his imperfections at once assembled in his recol-

lection, to convince him of his utter unworth-
iness of the Divine presence, and of the
miraculous power which had been exercised
in his behalf.

But Peter was not a common man. Raphael
has combined with the simplicity of an un-
taught individual the warm emotions and pro-
found qualities which were afterwards developed in the Apostle: his energy is subdued
by an extraordinary circumstance, but an
irresistible importunity of temperament is
revealed under the attitude of bended knees,
extended arms, and a countenance flexible to
every energetic and finer feeling. In the
midst of his consternation he discovers the
most sensible tenderness and attachment. Perhaps conscious of the infinite excellence and
unlimited power of the character before him,
he yields for a moment to the prevailing fear
of the Jews, of the danger of a superhuman
presence, but this is soon lost in different and
nobler feelings: the relation between him and

his Divine Master is, at this moment of miracle, alarm, and tenderness, at once and forever established.

Raphael has dressed this figure with his usual judgment. His plain garb of business, curly locks and beard, are highly characteristic, and help also to give additional dignity and grace to Christ, whose flowing and beautiful hair and superior attire invest him with those external advantages which ought to belong to his pre-eminent station.

Behind Peter is James. He also displays a most admirable feeling and expression. Homage, gratitude, and acknowledgment, are equally depicted in this graceful figure, whose ingenuous countenance shows the ease and readiness with which a grateful heart can pay its tribute, and invest with elegance of air and manner the humblest attitude of deference and respect: human obedience bowing to Divinity could not be more beautifully represented. He acquiesces in all that Peter

says and does, but has more dignity; he is
equally submissive, but is perhaps less pro-
foundly touched in those deep-seated emotions
which agitate a strong heart upon remarkable
occasions. At least it may be said he ranks
next to Peter, and is in every respect fitted
for his companion. The friendly fishermen
were afterwards associated Apostles.

The drapery of this figure is beautifully
adapted to its various forms, and the whole
finely relieved by the adjustment of its light
and shade.

The first character in the second boat is
John, whose person has not yet assumed those
graces which the special regard of Christ
shortly after this event communicated to him,
and rendered him in attraction next only to
his Master; his youth, however, is portrayed,
and his feelings indicated by the turn of his
head toward the principal scene. With the
ardor of a young man, he is determined to
make good the draught of the net, but cannot

deny himself the indulgence of his curiosity
in seeing how Peter and James were affected
by the miracle, and in what manner their
astonishment yields to devotion. In his exer-
tions he is seconded by Andrew, who strenu-
ously confines himself to his task; his wonder
is lost for the present in laborious and unexpected employment.

These stooping figures are finely drawn,
and by their position and attitude make an
interesting variety in the grouping.

At the end of this boat is Zebedee, care-
fully with his pole attending to the management of the vessel. Although the father of
James and John, he did not become one of the
distinguished twelve, and Raphael has not
therefore depicted in him a very striking
sensibility or quick consciousness of preternatural interposition: he has a fine countenance
and athletic form, but is the fisherman only.

Perhaps Raphael purposely confined the
great expression of his picture to the first

group : the attention is here excited to its
utmost power; some relief is necessary, and
the mind is gradually drawn off from this
splendid center of unrivaled design to the
scattered rays of expression and imagination
that lessen by degrees in the receding and
subordinate parts. After the secondary interest of the more distant boat, all is stillness and
repose : the peaceful lake receives the image
of the objects that are reflected on its surface,
the dim horizon melts into the air, the neighboring rocks ascend the sky, and a soft light
from above invests the whole with a serene
harmony of effect, that at once delights the
eye, gratifies the taste, and captivates the
heart.

After allusions to so many beauties, it is not
agreeable to descend to the consideration of
imputed faults; but so many observations
have been made on the dimensions and capacity of the boats, that it would, perhaps, excite

surprise to pass over this subject in silence; it would seem to imply either a contempt of a common opinion, or a hopelessness of rescuing the divine artist from its formidable censure. If to undertake the defense of Raphael, when it ought only to be required to admire him, be almost a reproach, the example of Richardson is offered as a justification.

The substance of his observation is as follows :—" The boats, perhaps, are too small, but this circumstance enabled Raphael to make his figures more conspicuous; vessels of a greater bulk would have ungracefully taken up the space, and something must have been sacrificed in the proportion of the figures to the other Cartoons."

Another author makes a pathetic appeal to candor, and thinks it almost impious not to overlook or deny trivial errors in men of splendid genius and established reputation.

These writers have omitted to remark, that Reubens, in one of his pictures representing

the same event, was so little conscious of dis-
proportion in the design, that in a boat of the
same capacity he has introduced five figures
instead of three.

The best apology, however, is the truth;
and if the mode be observed in which these
boats are built, it will be seen that the thick-
ness of the timbers renders them capable of
bearing the weight and containing the figures
allotted to them. They are rendered buoyant
by their massive substance, and boats of a
similar construction and size are still to be
seen on the coasts and rivers of Italy. Perhaps in the picture they seem shorter than
they actually are, because by some means the
ends of the cánvass have been narrowed. This
portion of the composition is replaced in the
engravings, by a reference to the copies of Sir
James Thornhill. It may be desirable to add,
to obviate another mistaken criticism regard-
ing the size of the birds, whose characteristic
introduction so materially assists the effect of

the picture, that travelers who have seen them in the East, describe them in color of a dark gray, and when at their full stretch about six feet in height.

VI.

PAUL AND BARNABAS REJECTING THE SACRIFICE AT LYSTRA.

Et hæc dicentes, vix sedaverunt turbas ne sibi immolarent.—Acts xiv. 18.

THE pre-eminent rule of looking to nature for examples and models, and of bringing back the imagination to her unerring government, when rendered irregular and intemperate by a too ardent pursuit of the sublime and beautiful of her works, was ever present to the mind of Raphael. He knew also that, although warmed with all the rays of genius, the richest invention would, by frequent efforts, become exhausted or languid, and that,

4

to counteract the lassitude which succeeds
every endeavor after perfection, it was necessary to keep the glorious object always in
view ; without which it is easy to be betrayed
into the spiritless toil of secondary excellence,
and to rest content with temporary praise.
He was rewarded for his vigilance and perse-
verance, by attaining the rank of unrivaled
master of the most captivating of arts. In
following with so much constancy his great
original, he not only acquired those essential
qualities of truth, dignity, and grace, which
constitute the loftier attributes of painting ;
but the talent of displaying endless variety in
the disposition of his groups, of expression and
attitude.

Thus Raphael's pictures, with their beautiful array of figures, show like fragments
snatched from the transitory living scenes of
the world, at the moment when they presented the most interesting combination of
circumstances. Characterized with whatever

is probable, and suitable to the event described, they are more than accompaniments
and illustrations of history ; they are in themselves records and evidences.

The meditated sacrifice at Lystra brought
into action many characters and occupations,
and excited great diversity of passions and
emotions. The city is agitated by an extraordinary occurrence ; wonder is attended with
fear, or with superstition, anger, or acquiescence, proselytism, or opposition.

It is related that the Apostles, Paul and
Barnabas, as they traversed the country of
Lycaonia, to disseminate the doctrines of
Christianity, made choice of an opportunity
at Lystra to confirm their mission by a
miracle.

There was a man who had been lame from
his birth, and who, in the hope of alms, was
undoubtedly placed in one of those public sit-
uations which the Apostles would naturally
select for their first address to the people.

"The same heard Paul speak : who steadfastly beholding him, and perceiving that he
had faith to be healed, said with a loud voice,
Stand upright on thy feet.   And he leaped
and walked."

This astonishing circumstance could not fail
to be immediately observed.   The rumor
spreads on every side ; a miracle cannot be
the work of human power ; "The gods are
come down in the likeness of men," is the ex-
clamation ; an idea which very naturally presented itself to the minds of the inhabitants of
Lycaonia ; a province so named from Lycaon,
one of the kings of this part of Asia, whose
history taught them that such an event was
not unprecedented.   St. Paul, as the chief
speaker, and on account of his eloquence, is
denominated Mercurius ; and Barnabas, Jupiter.   To the heavenly visitants, the honors of
the altar must be paid ; and the priests are
called on to perform the solemn office : "Then
the priest of Jupiter brought oxen and gar-

lands, and would have done sacrifice with the people."

It is easy to conceive the terrible agitation of the Apostles on finding themselves mistaken for those imaginary deities, and about to become the objects of that idolatrous worship, which they had hoped, by their conduct, and by the arguments and light of truth and knowledge, to destroy. Perhaps the very eloquence which had announced the mysterious incorporation of the Divine and human natures in that Being, whose sacrifice, embracing the universe in its intention, was designed to remove forever all living victims from the altar, and to close the portals, or reform the worship of every profane temple, became, in the minds of the ignorant or imperfectly enlightened, a partial confirmation of their own mythology. The Supreme, they were taught, had visited the earth in the form of man, and they could imagine no deity greater than Jupiter.

In the first ebullition of feeling thus produced, the Apostles vainly attempted to stay
the sacrificial preparations. They had recourse
to the most expressive language and gestures;
they rent their clothes, and ran in among the
people. Doubtless the eloquent and energetic
address of St. Paul must have prevailed with
many. "Why do ye these things? We also
are men of like passions with yourselves, and
preach unto you that ye should turn from
these vanities unto the living God." Notwithstanding, the general enthusiasm was at last
with difficulty controlled.

The picture represents St. Paul in the act of
rending his garments. The face of the Apostle is averted from a scene which he is afraid
to contemplate; his expression evinces disgust
and shame, humility and anger. Displeasure
and aversion are evident in his whole manner
and appearance : such perturbation must at
least show the most careless that he is far
from acquiescing in the extravagant and impi-

ous honors about to be celebrated. The drapery that invests this figure is magnificently
folded, and although copious, improves, rather
than conceals, the grace and vigor of the
form.

Barnabas, who is placed behind St. Paul,
suffers no less than the chief Apostle. In his
appeal to the people, he clasps his trembling
hands, and with devout and affecting supplication seems to implore the Divine Being for
deliverance of his servants from the evil of
which they were in danger of being made not
only the objects, but the innocent cause. The
look and deportment of Barnabas, so full of
meaning, communicate great solemnity to the
design. Who can forget the sublime purpose
of the Apostles, and the spirit in which they
came to instruct and convert the heathen,
when they behold a countenance and air re-
plete with piety and tenderness, benevolence
and purity, dignity and goodness? The extreme anxiety and alarm of this figure are

greatly increased in the expression by the raised heel; there can be no stronger external indication of inward emotion than such an action.

Meanwhile the intention of the inhabitants is not yet interrupted. The blow is about to fall with well-practiced certainty on the destined victim. The sacrificing priest, or Popa, with the axe, exerts his dexterous strength to the utmost; while his coadjutor, a priest of the same rank, one of whose offices is shown by the appendages attached to his girdle, fixes the animal by his nostrils, and watches the moment when to direct its fall at the foot of the altar.

The chief priest of Jupiter, the Flamen Dialis, whose temples are surrounded by the infula, a broad white bandage, stands next to the Popa with the uplifted axe. The Rex Sacrorum, another priest of dignity, officiates by his side. The young figure beyond is, by many, supposed to be a priestess: the expression and character of the features are feminine ; and as the wives of the superior priests were honored with titles derived from those of their husbands, the conjecture is reasonable that they sustained an occasional part in some of the religious services. The kneeling attendants close to the Popa with the dissecting instruments, are undoubtedly two of the Aruspices, whose duty it was to inspect the vitals of the slain animal, and examine the particular circumstances of the sacrifice, for the discovery of good or bad omens. The peculiar look and appearance of these officers strikingly suggest the idea of the soothsayer and diviner.

This part of the composition is probably an imitation of an antique basso-relievo; which in some respects it appears to resemble. Raphael perhaps judged that it was difficult to furnish a more perfect conception of a ceremony than its representation, executed by men of talent, at the time when it was frequently performed. In his desire to display an im-

4*

portant incident with minute truth, he thought
justly that, skillful adaptation was, on this occasion, preferable to the production of erring
novelty, however it might be recommended
by splendor or variety. In a few other in-
stances, Raphael did not disdain to take hints
from, and in part appropriate the invention of
others, when he could avail himself of origin-
als so well known as to protect him from the
charge of clandestine plagiarism ; and when
the appropriation was so excellent as fully to
meet his own ideas of what his scene required.

The rest of the picture conveys a most vivid
idea of a procession hastily formed, followed
by a tumultuous body every moment increasing in magnitude. In the rear all is motion
and agitation, and the numbers beginning to
press on those before. One individual only
has properly felt the impressive appeal of the
Apostles. He, like Abdiel, in single uncor-
ruptedness, passing from the hostile ranks of
the rebellious angels, " those proud towers to

swift destruction doomed," rushes forward
with irresistible force ; and with outstretched
arm and hand, that strives to reach its object,
endeavors to prevent the stroke. In this fine
figure are emphatically depicted passion of
feeling and swiftness of motion ; the face expresses intense anxiety ; and the eye, full of
fire and concern, at once pleads and com-
mands. Such is his impetuosity, that his
flowing hair flies behind, and exhibits to the
greatest advantage a countenance of animated
beauty. An interposition so powerful cannot
be unattended with its share of success. It
may be imagined, indeed, that the sacrificing
Popa has it yet in his power to suspend the
intended blow. A learned and distinguished
writer of the present day, with great critical
sagacity, has observed, that the right hand
seems suddenly carried toward the head of
the axe, in which situation alone it was possible to stay its descent.

Some commentators on the sacred text are

of opinion, that Timothy, the favorite convert
of St. Paul, was a native of Lystra, where it is
likely he received his first impressions of
Christianity; and, as it is evident from one of
the Epistles addressed to him by the Apostle, that this disciple was present at the perse-
cutions which he endured at Lystra, soon after
the intended sacrifice, Raphael, whose knowledge of divine history was complete, most
probably intended to represent Timothy in
the conspicuous figure just described. On
this supposition, the thought of introducing
him on such an occasion, endeavoring to second the wishes of his great teacher, cannot be
sufficiently admired. These graces of the pencil constitute in its highest degree what is
aptly termed the poetry of painting. The
praise bestowed by the lovers of Milton, on
the celebrated passage of his immortal work,
above alluded to, may with justice be equally
directed to this noble instance of pictorial
genius.

The expression of this figure not only affords a sublime interest to the subject, but displays, with increased effect, the sedate and demure characters of the priests near him, whose ceremonious and lifeless religion is, by their demeanor, well implied, and brought into contrast with the zeal and animation of a nobler inspiration.

In surveying the healed cripple, who occupies a chief situation in the picture, we easily perceive that his miraculous restoration is the cause of all this agitation. Nothing can exceed the cheerful gratitude, exultation, and joy of this character. We can imagine that he has been separated a moment, by the concussion or curiosity of the throng, from the presence of his benefactors, and, regaining sight of them, throws his loosened bandages and useless crutches to the ground, and hastens forward. His face, although coarse, is strongly expressive; with well-directed eye he fixes his glance on the Apostles; his raised

brow and open mouth show surprise as well as
delight. The manner of his advance and the
vigor of his step attest the perfectness of his
recovery. He is all alacrity and eagerness;
his hands, pressed together, are elevated, that
his gratitude may not escape notice. In the
confusion of his feelings, he scarcely considers
the absurd mistake of those about him in offering pagan honors to Christian teachers; he
thinks only that no homage which he is able
to pay can be too great to evince his sense of
the unexpected benefit which he has received.

It has been observed in a former Analysis,
that Raphael never dignifies his inferior characters with the features which denote superiority of mind or station. Whatever excep-
tions may be found, this is truly painting after
life. No longer lame, this man is still in appearance the public mendicant; his habits and
necessities are proved by his scanty and inferior attire, naked limbs, and tangled hair. He
cannot fail of remaining a sincere convert, but

he will always be among the humblest of the disciples.

The figure that immediately follows, presents a magnificent design; and is an admirable instance of the descriptive in painting. This elderly citizen, who appears, by his costly sandals and general exterior, to be an inhabitant of rank, seems, notwithstanding his age and dignity, to have impatiently hastened after and kept pace with the object of his curiosity; and, overtaking him at this moment, eagerly stoops and lifts up the skirt of the poor man's vest, to survey the restored limb. He beholds the cure with astonishment: his conviction of its reality and completeness is distinctly evinced by the action of his left hand: he perceives that the joints and muscles are not only sound, but vigorous, and that the very traces of infirmity have disappeared. The introduction of this noble character greatly dignifies the scene, and shows that the interest of the recent miracle was not confined to the humbler populace.

At the same time there are other exami-
nants : further in the group appear the expressive and finely-conceived faces of two spectators who are equally curious, and equally
gratified and convinced : there is a mixture of
considerable awe in their consciousness of the
supernatural power which has been exerted.
It is observed by an esteemed writer of the
preceding age, in allusion to the behavior of
the restored cripple, the discarded crutches,
and the manner of the three figures last noticed, that, to convey an understanding of the
scene, nothing could have been devised more
certain of the end proposed, and that such a
chain of circumstances is of itself almost an
elucidation of the subject.

The portly and self-important personage at
this extremity of the picture helps the idea of
a miscellaneous assembly ; in spite of his
haughtiness he is led away by the general interest, although cautious of manifesting it at
the expense of his consequence. He regards
the Apostles as if determined to make the

discovery of their characters for himself; but he is too content with his own dignity to indulge feelings of malevolence toward them, however averse to innovation, or surprised at the effects of a power which he cannot comprehend.

An appearance of still greater reality of life is given to this fine design by the contrasted faces and characters of the old and young female. The matron, whose look and action are remarkably significant, cannot control or disguise her feelings: her keen eye darts through the group, and regards the mysterious strangers not only with reverence, but the greatest admiration. The relief of the helpless creature, lately the object of general compassion, affords her a maternal satisfaction: so strong is the impulse of natural sympathy which governs her, that she elevates her hands in the same manner, and folds them with equal fervor.

Her juvenile and interesting companion has

the diffidence and hesitation of well-instructed
youth; she cannot in a moment resign herself
to appearances, or yield implicitly to first impressions. Unaccustomed to public occasions,
she equally restrains her joy and wonder; besides, although she looks with earnestness, and
is convinced of the dignity of the Apostles,
she cannot yet discover in them the imagined
youth and beauty of Mercury, or the sublime
majesty of the chief of the gods.

In order to keep up the idea of a two-fold
sacrifice, Raphael has introduced a party bringing a second ox: and to render the animal
conspicuous, seems to have exceeded the proper
proportion of his height. There is much natural representation in this group. One of the
conductors, in his zeal and haste, encroaches
on some who are not willing immediately to
remove. A spectator, perhaps a consul or
governor of the city, crowned with bay, turns
round, and as seen in all popular assemblies,
shows anger and resistance: but for the solem-

nity of the proceeding, the proud Roman would resent the affront of being obliged to remove from his station.

In the foreground, the scene is greatly diversified. Two beautiful children, trained in uncontaminated innocence, lend their well-taught aid to the solemn service. One, a Camillus, holds the Thurarium, or incense-box, ready to perfume the flames which rise from the richly-decorated altar. The other, a Tibicen, whose minstrelsy also commanded the attention of the people, and diverted the ear from other sounds, with modest yet earnest simplicity, breathes through his two-fold pipe the notes of praise.

The last figure to notice is the athletic individual who brings the ram; and who, although mindful of his duty, turns his head with respectful timidity towards St. Paul, as if surprised at his actions. He is probably one of the Victimarii, who had the charge of providing and properly preparing the animals required for sacrifice. Like the other attendants, a garland adorns his head, and his appearance is of great use to give completeness to the effect of a public festival and sacrifice. This part of the picture wanted, besides, a figure of large proportions, in order to give distance to the Apostles, without concealing them too much; which would have been the effect of a group: with this view, the ram is added, that by the necessity of holding the animal, advantage might be taken of a stooping attitude.

Raphael has communicated dignity to his subject by placing his scene in the center of public buildings of splendid architecture. The temple of Jupiter is on the left, and affords a commanding situation to the Apostles. That of Mercury is at a distance, and is indicated by his statue.

The whole is a composition truly classical. The chief intention was to represent the noble and affecting passion of St. Paul and Barnabas: this, therefore, is the most impressive part of the design : here is its surpassing greatness. The rest is explanatory, and abounds, indeed, with strong and proper interest, and beauties of the highest order : but while we survey with delight the well-depicted joy and elastic vigor of sudden health, the pomp of sacrifice, and the agitation of a multitude, we cannot be insensible to a deeper feeling, on comparing with these exhibitions, the over-whelming distress of humility, apprehension, and indignation, felt by men brought up under the imprescriptible law, "Thou shalt have none other gods but me," who not only witness a gross violation of that law, occasioned by a misconception of what they had themselves instrumentally performed, but perceive their own persons about to be deified and adored. Such subjects demand the utmost power of the pencil: and it is not paying his immortal memory too much honor to affirm, that Raphael alone has been found capable of doing them perfect justice.

NOTE.

Some critics have observed on the figure of Barnabas, that, as this Apostle was distinguished by the natives of Lystra with the appellation of Jupiter, he must have appeared a man of great personal dignity and commanding stature; and that Raphael, therefore, has failed to represent him correctly. To this remark it may be replied, that, had Barnabas been too eminently prominent in the design, St. Paul would have taken the place of a secondary figure; and this Apostle was doubtless intended to be the hero of the picture; which, as the chief actor in the scene, he ought to be. In the same style of criticism it might be urged, that some resemblance of the youthful beauty and activity of Mercury should have characterized St. Paul, which qualities, it must be owned, are not even indicated. Raphael had higher objects: it was not his purpose to represent heathen deities, but Christian Apostles. Besides, he considered, perhaps, that St. Paul and Barnabas were severally designated Jupiter and Mercurius, not because of their external appearance, but because of the power they had displayed; and because these were the gods of the city to whom the chief worship was paid.

VII.

THE

BEAUTIFUL GATE OF THE TEMPLE.

———•••———

IF the distinction of superior praise ought
to be admitted in favor of this noble Cartoon,
which has frequently been considered one of
the most attractive of the series, it does not
arise from its subject as the representation of
a miracle. "The Beautiful Gate of the Temple" communicates ideas, rather than exhibits
striking external movement, and requires
study as well as refined feeling to be fully ap-
preciated: it is a quiet development of pre-

ternatural interposition, in which Raphael has
not attempted to describe the numerous re-
sults that would attend such an event if pub-
licly announced, or previously expected. Had
the imagination of this great artist not de-
ferred to his judgment and his knowledge, he
might have introduced many remarkable di-
versities of passion and emotion, characteristic
of different conditions, temperaments, and
ages, on mixed occasions of solemn excitement
and tumultuous wonder; and to that just and
reflective admiration which his work, in its
present form, will ever create, would be added
the effect of immediate surprise, and the animated interest of a more eager curiosity.
But Raphael was faithful to the history, and
could not have failed to observe generally
that, in the promulgation and establishment
of Christianity, the Apostles did not aim at
conquering the minds of men by preconcerted
manifestations of power, delegated to them as
well for the conscious sanction of their mis-

sion as its outward witness. The heavenly
light that was destined to shed eternal radi-
ance on the moral scene, and assist the human
wanderer in the labyrinth of error in his escape from its dark mazes, would, by boundless
effusion of insupportable splendor suddenly
shining upon him, have dazzled and obscured
the mental vision, and left him bewildered
and involved in deeper shade. The object of
the Apostles was to imbue the masses of mankind with a conviction of the truth of their
sacred cause by the force or gradual operation
of its own evidence, and by their personal example of goodness and usefulness; and although, at intervals, impelled by overruling
motives to combine, but never ostentatiously,
the support and confirmation of superhuman
actions, rested their success, under Divine direction and assistance, chiefly on natural principles.

It is the illustration of this practical part
of the Apostolic plan that constitutes the pre-

vailing and enduring charm which pervades
the present correct composition. Raphael was
minutely acquainted with the philosophy of
the mental structure; and, with unerring skill
of adaptation, availed himself of those uni-
versal ideas of beauty, greatness, goodness,
which are early associated in the mind, and
are always present when not obstructed by
hostile prejudices and passions, or external interruption. He was aware that it is by their
ceaseless, although often unperceived, vigilance and activity that we are delighted, astonished, affected; and that, in proportion as
we justly estimate the objects to which they
relate, the taste is refined, the understanding
enlarged, and the heart improved. In the
adoption of these unfailing means of art, in
the present instance, he exerted his genius
with the greater ardor, having to introduce
opposing but not discordant images, which,
with infinite address, he has reconciled to the
general design, and made to increase the pre-

dominate interest by calling into exercise collateral principles and congenial feelings, and thus disclosing a wider prospect over the varied empire of sensitive and intelligent nature. This digression may, it is hoped, be allowed, as it will be found to apply, in many places, to the assumed superiority of a cartoon, in which all that is beautiful, and great, and good, is depicted. Yielding to its fascination, we soon discover presented to our notice the dignity of authority and power, the grace of charity and kindness ; and while the attention is deeply engaged by the clearly indicated accomplishment of a miracle, our hearts and sympathies are irresistibly won by the expression and demeanor of the inspired agents. The impressive scene immediately acts on the moral observation, and suggests the reflection that to benevolence and goodness an attribute bordering on the miraculous is still granted, to whose aid defective or afflicted nature appeals not in vain. Through their instrumentality he that was lame walks; the blind, once more surveying all things with delight, rejoin the busy throng; or, if doomed to the calamity of organic darkness, languish not in idleness and privation, but learn the useful arts and industry which belong to sight; and they whose ear is silence, and without voice their breath, are taught to understand and to reciprocate knowledge. Their preceptive and consolatory influence is equally, with their actions, blessed in the mitigation of irremediable ills, and in imparting to the hopeless sufferer the alleviation of patient submission to the Sovereign Will.

How diligently Raphael studied the sacred text, which narrates the incident now represented, is apparent. The Apostles Peter and John were entering the temple at Jerusalem by the " Gate which was called Beautiful ; " a cripple who was brought there daily, and had been lame from his birth, solicited alms as they passed: "Then Peter said, Silver and gold have I none, but such as I have I give unto thee; in the name of Jesus of Nazareth, rise up and walk." There are in this short history, of which the preceding is an irregular extract, many circumstances peculiarly calculated to affect and improve the feelings. The sentiment expressed by St. Peter, before the miracle, is beautiful: it is not possible, by any other language, to convey so vivid an idea of a good and kind heart. "Silver and gold have I none,"—the Apostle would have added, if he had not known what better gifts he was able to bestow, "would that I possessed these treasures, that I might gratify thy importunity with alms." It is evident the consciousness of Divine inspiration had come upon him at the first sight of the cripple; but there was no visible demonstration to show his sublime purpose toward him, nor did he attempt to inflame his mind by the infusion of enthusiasm, or exhortations of confidence: his attention had been summoned only by the dignified command, "Look on us!"

To St. Peter is assigned a prominent part in four Cartoons. At first he is represented as disciple and fisher. The union is easily traced : there is an expressive greatness even in his humility and perturbation, which attests the sincerity and zeal, the fervor and affectionate disposition, of his ingenious nature. The language he adopted, at this time, in the solitude of that holy isolation, which was the scene of the miracle, is interpreted by the picture with intense fidelity. Here St. Peter gains our esteem. The Cartoon of Christ's appearance after his resurrection also powerfully impresses his character on our regard. He is again kneeling, but in the more quiescent posture of attention and suspense, which preceded the period of his impassioned confession and assurance : his agitation was at first concealed. In what other attitude more suited to the remembrance of his recent defection could he listen to that affecting appeal and address, which at once contained the words of reproof and intended reconciliation ? From this solemn communion of penitence and forgiveness, of grief, renewed attachment, and confidence, St. Peter rises infinitely exalted by his reappointment to the pastoral office. In the Cartoon of Ananias, the Apostle, having passed through all his probations, is seen with great exterior dignity. The important and benevolent purpose which now assembled him with his associates was abruptly suspended by the conduct of an impostor, who dared to profane their gracious administration by an act of deliberate and impious hypocrisy, which, in a moment, converted the apostolic body into a holy court of retributive judicature. In this august reunion, St. Peter, who is readily distinguished as the supreme judge, shows, in his suddenly altered aspect, the energy of that awful reproof which he addressed to the guilty dissembler, and which, by the terrible force of its application to his alarmed conscience, was, it is not improbable, alone sufficient to cause the fatal issue of his premeditated crime.

To our constantly increasing esteem and regard for St. Peter, respect and homage are
now added. His fourth introduction, not in
the order of history, but in relation to this
work, is in the picture at present to be exam-
ined. The humble disciple, the majestic organ of judicial punishment, and the benevolent Apostle, here form one character. The
combination is perfect. Who, on surveying the
noble figure before him, would wish, in pre-
ference, any other guide and instructor, any
other friend and benefactor? How parental
his expression, how dignified his air and features, how mildly authoritative, how serenely
powerful! he stretches forth his hand, and
the object of his beneficence is healed.

Raphael has devoted particular study to
this delineation, of which all the parts har-
moniously accord : the head, the hands, the
foot, display a corresponding style of true
greatness : and the drapery which envelops
the Apostle is copious, grand, and beautiful.

Nothing more can be desired to furnish the imagination with a just and permanent idea of St. Peter.

Next to the principal actor in this scene is the amiable St. John, whose name alone suffices to gain the attention and awaken our prepossessions. The design is instantly recognized ; and, while admirably contrasted with the preceding figure, reinforces the impression already created. The goodness, the moral ascendancy, the consciousness of Divine endowment, the benevolence, are equal. There is a perfect participation in the same purpose. Such a union of exalted qualities and virtues would have produced a favorable effect on the mendicant, even if the miracle had not been permitted. Yet the youth of St. John, his beauty, his natural mildness of disposition, his grace, considerably heighten the previous interest which now possesses the whole mind. It is difficult to observe that fine countenance, which discloses compassion almost approaching to pain, a pity that afflicts the bosom from which it springs, without partaking these emotions. St. John, it is plain, had heard the voice of earnest supplication, and regarded unpretending distress with deep commiseration, before he perceived the intention of his associate.

With what rapidity are communicated the sentiments and impulses of goodness! but the sacred energy simultaneously descended on each Apostle: the miracle performed was the act of both. Raphael has described this co-operation by the manner of St. John, whose ready hand eloquently shows the sincerity, the ardor of his cordial concurrence, while it is directed with the native grace of kindness, and with persuasive encouragement, toward the humble expectant. No further aid is required by him who has already felt a pressure which will restore his limbs to soundness and renovate his depressed mind.

The entire appearance of this favored minister of heaven is extremely engaging; his features are regular as well as expressive;

the hair, so significant of his character, flowing
and ornamental. The latter appendage Raphael never neglected in any of his principal
heads ; especially not in the delineation of the
youngest of the Apostles ; of which remark
the " Charge to Peter " affords ample confirmation. The importance Raphael assigned to
this personal recommendation calls to mind
the animated apostrophe of the amiable
and philosophic Lavater, who exclaimed, on
surveying a celebrated portrait, " it is enough
to see thy beautiful hair to admire thee, and
be convinced of thy virtues !" The finely
arranged mantle of the Apostle invests him
with external majesty and grace : and the
tunic is a little depressed, that the eye may
decline, a moment, on that gentle bosom which,
more than any other, was imbued with Divine
love and human tenderness. This little accessory is a pleasing and appropriate symbol of
youth and innocence, and completes the representation of St. John.

It is difficult to take leave of these transcendent figures of the Apostles without a retrospective glance at many circumstances in their eventful history. They may justly be considered as resembling men who were long in the company of Him who took precedence over all mankind in the sanctity of his life, and the authority of his mission : with whom they were present in the glory of his transfiguration, and by whose side they stood when he rendered sorrow and humanity forever sacred by his lamentation over the impending fate of Jerusalem. All the purity, the sublimity, the practice, the effect, of true religion are united in these examples. All that can exalt the mortal, or reveal the immortal, as far as visible things can be the mirror of those which are eternal, or that can connect this lowly state of frail and transitory existence with the imperishable principle which carries the mind far into the heaven of heavens toward its holy origin, permitted and encouraged in its aspirations after infinite perfection by Him who made it in his image, is here, on

the threshold of his own sanctuary, impressed
on the understanding and the heart with the
uttermost force of moral instruction. Raphael,
who meditated whatever affects, and elevates,
and teaches, in the inspired page, and so intel-
ligibly transmitted his ideas, thus sacredly derived, into his scriptural paintings, that they
became an auxiliary school of divinity, has
surpassed all his other efforts in these two
chief characters of this subject. It is not sentiment alone, nor poetic fancy, nor profitless
enthusiasm, which are elicited; it is Truth, that
through the lucid veil of pictorial forms, and
combinations, and expression, persuasively in-
vites to the contemplation of her majesty, and
enforces obedience to her supreme influence,
while she offers the example and proclaims
the relative and inviolable duties of humanity
and piety. In this manner Raphael raised his
art into a science of the highest order !

The attention reluctantly, perhaps, de-
scends to the forlorn being beneath: but the

exhibition is alike necessary to the scene and
to connect the ideas of kindness and charity
with their natural causes of pain and want;
and to show, at once, the virtue, and its object.
The alliance is, indeed, intimate; and is here
revealed with inimitable pathos of expression
and grandeur of action.   The hand of the
Apostle is in immediate union with humble
wretchedness,—how wide is the separation of
their condition; how indissoluble the affinity
of their nature!   Philanthropy is a flower
which shoots from the dark earth moistened
by the ceaseless springs of affliction: expand-
ing and beautiful in the ray of prosperity, it
perceives and tells its origins when, drooping,
it looks toward the ground encumbered with
the dew of pity.   It is not given to be severed
from its stem, awhile to adorn the cold bosom
of heartless sentiment, or to languish in the
glittering vase of idle sensibility; but to
bloom in permanent and perennial glory, shed-
ding odors on its native bed.

The humble character now to be described is not the lowest of his class. It is true, the man who lives by his miseries must, apparently, become abject and degraded; yet we see also, in the striking example before us, a candidate for the public bounty through unavoidable necessity, whose indigence is without depravity. His pallid countenance, which is imprinted with the not unfrequently united traits of affliction and content, shows that alms have generally been presented to him with a cheerful hand, and received, as charity ought always to be received, with a grateful heart. On a closer consideration of his expression, we may observe, notwithstanding his confidence in the Apostle, in whose power he evidently is, and whose solemn adjuration and gracious promise have wrought in him mingled astonishment and hope, a slightly anxious look of apprehended pain or violence in his expected recovery: at least, he seems doubtful whether to shrink in fear, or yield with joy,

under a new and awful influence, equally irresistible as beneficial. St. Peter may be supposed to have perceived this natural terror ;
and, judging by his calm, collected attitude,
in which self-possession, energy, and gentleness are consummately blended, may allow an
instant to elapse for the timid sufferer to conceive the mental image of his approaching
change, and to feel the vigor of his upper
frame vibrate toward the lower extremities.
The moment has passed ; and the spectator,
in idea, beholds the recent cripple erect on
limbs of strength, elasticity, and proportion.
It is easy to imagine the benign aspect of his
benefactors, and the boundless joy and gratitude of the restored, which immediately followed the miracle. How appositely, in this
place, does the interesting sequel of the story
recur to the memory : "and he, leaping up,
stood and walked, and entered, with the
Apostles, into the temple, walking, and leaping, and praising God !"

Raphael has judiciously thrown a deep shadow over the feet of the cripple, that, while his lameness is sufficiently discovered on examination, it may not engage the first notice too obtrusively.

This entire group, in marble, would be a superb ornament in the area of one of those numerous edifices, whose doors are gratuitously open night and day to natural or accidental infirmity and misfortune, and which constitute the noblest embellishments of great cities. The sculptor who could succeed in embodying with precision these three figures, would confer signal honor on himself and on the country to which he might present his splendid, and equally original, as imitative, work.

The introduction of the second deformed mendicant may, possibly, by some, be considered superfluous: it therefore demands a short enquiry. Perhaps Raphael anticipated that the observer, pleased and satisfied with the preceding restoration, might be disposed too hastily to dismiss from reflection the image of pain, and with it the corresponding sentiment of sympathy. It was his wish, on the contrary, to check this sudden transition, and to hint, with the moralist, "thou hast relieved one,—there are many who require thy assistance!" an admonition which brings to the memory that most expressive, instructive, and useful exhortation, "Be not weary in well-doing."

Raphael did not forget that, at the time of this event, as in his own day, poverty and misery had no home; and were succored, not by the obligation of law, but by the rule of voluntary and habitual kindness. It was a worthy effort, on his part, to stimulate and render permanent the best qualities of our nature. Besides, as the principal entrance of the temple was likely to be the chief resort of the afflicted, a solitary object of compassion would not convey an adequate idea of the scene as it really existed. Raphael, therefore,

on this occasion, justifies the remark that, it is
his adherence to what is probable, as well as
natural, which contributes so greatly to the
success of his exhibitions of history.

Pictorially considered, this part of the
composition required a design that would not
injuriously intercept the adjacent figures ; and
if, for the sake, only, of diversity, Raphael
had represented a less painful spectacle, he
might have incurred the hazard of a fault,
which, it may be thought, escaped the observation of the late Mr. West, in his magnificent
picture of " Christ healing the Sick." The
criticism will not offend ; and if, while capti-
vated by the numerous beauties of that
admired work, we are, for a moment, drawn
away from the invalid, who is the immediate
object of the power of Christ, to the affecting
appearance of the blind female on the left,
the error is redeemed by the pathos of this
most touching appeal to the feelings. It is
possible, also, that Raphael, superlatively the

painter of grace and dignity, might have been inclined to prove, when his subject would permit, that he was equally able to depict their contraries; and that life and nature were known to him in all their infinitely varied forms and conditions. This conjecture calls forth the idea of another vast and parallel genius, that master-mind, which at one time presented the exquisitely conceived character of Ophelia, "the young, the beautiful, the harmless, and the pious;" and, in another celebrated drama, exhibited a Caliban, shapeless, monstrous, savage, and depraved. Whatever the motive of Raphael might be, the design in question is true to the state of extreme and long-dependent poverty.

It is difficult to judge accurately of the expression of this inferior man : he does not seem malignantly opposed to the Apostles, or envious of his late associate in calamity, if indeed he is able to comprehend the meaning of the promised boon : but he is, plainly, a mendicant by choice, and is furnished for his occasional necessities; he can change his place without help, and lives by his infirmities; he is even now thinking of alms, and would not, perhaps, without admonition and entreaty, prefer a perfect cure of his deformities to the gifts of "silver and gold."

Next to the Apostle John is seen a dignified personage, who, with well-marked self-possession, and a countenance of the purest philanthropy, awaits the issue of the scene near him, which he observes attentively: he will not hastily reject, nor incautiously anticipate, the evidence of a remarkable occurrence; when convinced he will retain his conviction. He is one of those superior characters who are to be found in every better order of society, whose sole and constant objects are to learn what is useful, and practice what is good.

The head, partly concealed by the pillar, is of use to the composition, chiefly as it displays strong and mixed expression, and thus helps to keep in view the momentous interest of the subject, and as offering a contrast to the rest of the group. The head is left somewhat unfinished in the Cartoon, as if Raphael had not quite decided on his intention. A young person of lively feeling once observed, that the countenance is that of a vicious atheist, who felt himself in sudden danger of being overwhelmed with shame by the force of irresistible evidence, and of becoming the scorn and derision of many whom he had misled by premeditated perversions of truth. There is certainly a vacant stare in his face characteristic of the "fool who hath said in his heart, there is no God."

The fine old man near the cripple deserves particular notice. With the quickest penetration into the meaning of the scene, he has thrown himself into his accustomed attitude, whenever any remarkable circumstance engages his attention. He rests firmly on his staff, and, with keen and inquisitive eye, ap-

pears to expect in the countenance of St.
Peter some new and mysterious manifestation
of Divine power, beyond the benignant regard
and energy of mere human expression. So
fixed is his scrutinizing look, and so firm his
purpose, that neither is he deterred by the
impetuosity of the individual behind him,
who is endeavoring to force his way forward,
nor by the thoughtless violence of the boy,
his grandson, as may be supposed by the confident familiarity of his action, who, with no
puny strength, draws him by the girdle, and
seems to say, " Let us depart into the temple ;
do you not see my mother and my brother
hastening thither ? "

Raphael has clearly intended in this head
to discriminate the striking individuality of
Jewish features; it is elaborately finished, and
will, in all respects, bear a comparison with
the finest heads of Lionardo da Vinci, who in
his chef d'œuvre of the " Last Supper," determined by a similar motive, has, perhaps,

carried these characteristics a little beyond
the usual limit of nature.

A picture can only properly represent one
moment of time; but we may imagine the
enthusiasm of this venerable citizen, after the
miraculous cure, when, forgetting his age and
infirmities, he will evince his amazement by
uplifted hands, eyes sparkling with new fire,
open mouth, and interrupted breath, alter-
nately fixing his gaze on the Apostles and the
healed man, and then exerting the utmost of
his remaining vigor to rejoin, within the sacred edifice, the song of praise issuing from
many voices!

The figure before alluded to, pressing forward, is finely conceived; it is altogether
Raphaelian. The animation and direct progress of his movement through the obstructing
group, contribute materially to the interest of
the scene, which, without this aid, might
appear too tranquil and isolated. He regards
not the rules of courtesy; he has heard some-

thing that engrosses all his thoughts, and he will for himself know the result of the mysterious annunciation of the Apostle. The position of the head, upraised shoulder, and eager manner, all correspond to denote his resolute curiosity.

There is another head in this division of the picture which is a fine, although not a prominent, design.

How majestically, on the right, stands the noble figure, partly concealed by the mendicant and the front, pillar, of the most dignified spectator in the composition! How masculine, and yet how elegant his form and attitude! how express his action! His superior capacity and mental energy are no less conspicuous than his exterior advantages. The feelings which agitate him are easily disentangled; although naturally irascible, he would be gratified at the performance of merely human benevolence; but not entirely persuaded of the Divine endowments of these Christian

6

teachers, he thinks there is an assumption in
the language and _manner of St. Peter, and
imputes to him a too confident use of the
name of one whom he knows is esteemed
sacred by a large proportion of the people.
His stern determination not to approach the
Apostles, implies an hostility toward them
which he is neither able nor inclined to re-
press. He has himself authority in the temple, and, jealous of his distinction, apprehends
some new disclosure of their power, by which
he may suffer humiliation. • He fears also another inroad on the stability of those ancient
institutions of which he is a servant, and
whose influence has already been weakened
by many remarkable recent events, and by
new interpretations of the law connected with
them. In the elevation of his left hand, he
unconsciously imitates St. Peter; it is the
natural effect of a deeply-interested and fixed
observance of another's motions, and is equally
significant of hope and fear. This personage

also greatly promotes the animation and unity of the design.

Beyond, in shade befitting his character and purpose, is one who, by disposition a scorner of truth and virtue, is, by occupation, a spy of the worst description. His instructions are to observe minutely, and relate correctly; but, although he sees all that is good and right, he will report only evil. He will not come near, that he may not be deterred, by irrefragable evidence against him, from his projected falsehoods. The less he discovers the more he can invent: he wants only the groundwork of his information; he knows that general and vague testimony can be more easily, and will be more readily, supported, than faithful and exact details, by witnesses who commonly recollect what is most prominent, and whose consciences are, therefore, not expressly engaged on the side of truth. This artful intruder is abandoned, not only to prejudice,

but to malice: he has no contrition, and is
identified with his profession: were he not
employed and paid he would be a volunteer
in his bad office.

Gladly does the eye remove from his for-
bidding aspect, to the captivating display of
grace, innocence, and beauty, of the Jewish
female, who, with her infant in her arms, is
returning from the interior of the temple.
The disapprobation and disgust which, in the
preceding survey, began to darken the imagination with painful reflections, are dissipated
at the first glance of so amiable an object, and
we are again restored to that more agreeable
estimate of human nature, which is as beneficial as it is encouraging. The attention of
this pious mother is arrested, as she gently
steps forward, by a spectacle perfectly in harmony with her disposition. Her mind is in
the most delightful state; still dwelling on
the recent exercise of her devotions at the
altar, where, with sincerity and cheerfulness,

she performed, at once, the duties of the law and of inclination. She is a consistent votary, and we may suppose had entered the temple distributing alms liberally, to him especially who is now the subject of Apostolic aid; receiving, in exchange, looks and words of benediction and gratitude. She is grateful for herself, for her first-born, for whom she has been offering up gifts and thanks; and who has been solemnly dedicated a new member of the religion of her forefathers. The most pleasing of all cares occupy her thoughts, to which, with graceful delicacy of unconscious motion, her gentle hand modestly responds; yet is she sufficiently disengaged to yield to emotions arising from another's benefit. The character is a faultless model of propriety of mien and behavior. Raphael perceived the value of his idea, and added the accessories of a rich and noble dress, and costly ornaments. These elegant decorations, and the tasteful arrangement of her hair, denote her wealth and superior station; which are, besides, appropriately hinted by the company of her attendant, whose presence fills up a scene of natural and maternal loveliness with the customary decorum of social distinction.

The attention 'now deviates to the other side of the picture. It is not easy to say which of the two designs of feminine perfection is the more justly entitled to our admiration; yet these delightful creations of art are essentially different in character and manner. We turn from the sober pace of the recent mother, the placid yet penetrating glance of her dark and compassionate eye, naturally expressive of the sweetest sensibility, to the liveliness of blooming health, and the alacrity of purpose which accelerate the progress of the female, bearing a basket of offerings on her head, and conducting by the hand her little son, whose beauty and swiftness of foot, as running he keeps close to her side, animate her with becoming pride. All the elegance that can attend celerity of movement, and the grace and buoyant lightness of the elastic step of youth invigorated by a virtuous object, and accustomed to praise, distinguish her charming figure. She passes like light and air through the canvass; and the tranquility we before felt is now exchanged for sentiments in harmony with this most interesting personification of parental vivacity. She must not be deemed one of that reprehensible number who, betrayed by the impatient desire of gain, often leaves the precincts, and sacrilegiously advance within the sacred edifice to barter doves for silver; the various gifts she takes are for herself and family, not for profit. Her looks are those of sincere and habitual religious obedience, and she is happy and cheerful because she is good and grateful.

The beauties of this design are so obvious, that it is scarcely necessary to invite the attention to it minutely. The form itself, the motion of the arms, the turn of the head, the

evanescent drapery, the exquisite light and
shade, the identity of parent and child, whose
simplicity, and innocence, and participation
of movement are so attractively depicted, all
combine to constitute an accessory to the
main action of the picture, which can never
be surpassed in the delight it affords the spectator, and in its appositeness to the locality
of the scene.

Beyond, veiled by the shadow of the
building, are two figures equally applicable
to this locality. These appear waiting for a
convenient time to enter the temple for devo-
tional purposes, to which the female is probably led by the natural impulse of a pious
mind impressed, as may be imagined, with
thoughts of the maternal future.

Raphael has here evinced his usual knowledge of incidental expression. With feminine
softness there are united a solemnity and pen-
sive abstractedness, visible in all whose pros-
pects are divided between that confidence

and alternate doubt which accompany the consideration of an important event yet at a distance. Her husband yields to similar reflections; and the group resembles the sentimental character of many of the numerous pictures of the Holy Family.

It must be borne in mind that, although the Messiah had appeared and accomplished his great work, yet the majority of the Jewish people, being disappointed in their expectation of a pageant of human glory that should surpass in magnificence and success all the triumphs which had hitherto awed and dazzled the world, looked forward with unabated confidence to the fulfillment of this ardently cherished prediction of national deliverance from bondage and subsequent aggrandizement of power. Their uncontrolled imagination still continued to dwell on the near advent of an irresistible leader to victory, a legislator greater than Moses, a prophet without an equal in their recorded annals of prophetic renown, and

6*

a king of a renovated kingdom, ordained to rest on the eternal decree and protection of the Supreme Being, before whose word all nations were to be dissolved, or forever subdued to the throne of David. The married Jewess, therefore, often entertained the solemn hope that she might be honored with this mysterious nativity; and so hallowed a reliance on heavenly favor conferred evident dignity on the marriages of the pious part of the Jewish community.

Raphael was conscious of the greatness of. his talents; he doubted not that his pictures were destined not merely to please the eye for the recreation of an hour, but to accompany history, and permanently to engross the mind of all who possessed taste, judgment, and knowledge. He was convinced that, deeply and irresistibly detained by the chief purpose of his composition, it would, so enlarged and imbued with kindred ideas, travel through its remotest parts, and not desist till the entire scope of his comprehensive plan became apparent and fully understood.

The introduction of the naked children requires some investigation. It is probable that Raphael, perceiving the necessity of depicting deformities that ought to be strongly marked in order to magnify the miracle of their cure, and to create a proper feeling of compassion, involuntarily turned back his imagination to the ideal of nature's perfect work; to which, it is obvious, the prevailing bias of his genius ever inclined. The beauty, harmony, and magnificence of the creation, commensurate with which in extent and excellence expanded his perceptions of its moral government, constituted the sphere in the midst of whose equal attraction his mind, glowing with their communicated attributes, centered; and, from this lofty and serene intellectual eminence of light and inspiration, descended the reflected glory of his immortal productions. He had, indeed, surrounded a

humiliating exhibition with many forms of
dignity and grace, as they usually appear in
the living scene; but, unclothed limbs, dis-
torted by disease and accident, could only be
contrasted by the display of similar parts of
the body framed in health, vigor, and proportion. Statues could not find a place in the
composition without making it too artificial;
neither, under any arrangement of the architecture, would they be admissible in a Jewish
subject. The only alternative, therefore, was
the delineation of nature in her earlier stages
of life. The boy in front exactly corresponds
with this conjecture, and discovers the muscles of the human fabric adequately developed
by the playful exertion of juvenile impatience.
Free from all embarrassment, arms, head, and
legs, show a flexibility of motion and energy
of conformation resembling the more mature
and heroic models which were selected for
the sculptures of the Grecian artists, when,
ambitious to adorn the splendid temples of

their nation, they aimed at displaying forms
worthy to represent the divinities of their
fabled heaven. The younger child, in a different view, is graceful as the former is athletic; animated and delighted with his pleasing office, with which he is charged, perhaps,
for the first time, of carrying on his shoulder
a pair of doves, apt emblems of his own innocence, he follows his careful conductress with
his utmost activity, and his swift pace gave
Raphael the opportunity he desired of describing the free and unrestrained motion of
progress as well as local action. A secondary
object in the introduction of these children
was, it appears, to prevent the numerous pil-
lars from attracting the eye by too many suc-
cessions of equal light, which, necessarily mo-
notonous, might otherwise have prevailed
over the important parts of the picture which
ought to be prominent. The figures of the
children could not fail to restore the proper
adjustment of the general harmony of effect

by their adaptation to receive on their polished surfaces reflection equal to that glancing
from the sculptured marble.

The ornamental part of the picture is im-
posing and interesting. Raphael's purpose
was to present a beautiful vestibule in accord-
ance with the epithet in the text: and not,
perhaps, being able, without great research,
to conform to the example of ancient Jewish
architecture, gave the reins to his invention,
in order that he might atone for the neglect
of strict propriety by elegance of design and
embellishment, and by the charm of novelty.
He has done entire justice to his determination. The general plan is magnificent; the
curvilinear elevation of the columns graceful;
the flutings and moldings highly finished;
the imitative foliage tasteful; and the sport-
ive effusions of his pencil in the delightful
and numerous sculptures of cupid-like children in every variety of attitude, some reach-
ing at the clustering treasures of the vine, and

others in pursuit of the glittering butterfly, complete his conception of an exhibition addressed, not to the judgment, but to the fancy.

On the left, the landscape is visible beyond the sacred structure. He who has wandered, as, doubtless, Raphael often wandered, amongst the majestic ruins of ancient Rome, or, with arrested step pausing to contemplate those sublime edifices which the force of ages has spared amidst the scattered fragments and dust of meaner structures and the dwellings of man, has been suddenly dazzled by the rising or setting sun, darting its rays through open spaces of dilapidated walls and solitary columns, or has been charmed by the blue summit of distant hills seen beneath the curve of the triumphal arch, will not be surprised at this license of the painter. It was of no consequence to his subject to convey the idea of a central and incumbered situation of the temple, but it was necessary to suit the per-

spective scenery to the effect which he
thought best adapted to the local airiness or
the substantial richness of the general design.
The landscape openings afford a pleasing and
skillful contrast to the solemn shade under the
principal portico, which forms a still and deep
relief to the figures connected with the scene
of the miracle. But the opposition is not
abrupt: the soft light of the distant sky is
succeeded by the trembling flame of pendant
lamps, which, burning from the morning to
the evening twilight, gently dispel the gloom
of deep intablatures and reduplicated columns.
Besides this use of these scattered scintilla-
tions, Raphael intended, probably, to unite
the idea of sanctity with magnificence, by the
adoption of emblems considered by all nations
significant of the purity, warmth, and constancy, of religious devotion.

On a general review of this favorite Cartoon, its copious and miscellaneous character,
throughout applicable to the importance of

the sacred history which it illustrates, will easily be discovered. It comprehends an extensive range of life and nature. The affecting survey brings to memory that noble introductory line of a Grecian drama, which made its author and declaimer famous: "I am a man, and therefore deeply feel all that relates to man." The picture furnishes an enlarged comment on this sentiment. In expression it commences with that almost imperceptible agitation which immediately succeeds perfect serenity, and proceeds to the stronger delineation of the passions, to the surprise, the hope, the terror, of an impending miracle. Its objective scenery in the gradual development of progressive life possesses great interest. The infant reposes softly on the bosom of maternal love ; the running child clings to the parent hand ; the boy, of active and self-dependent strength, exerts his playful force, and by his animation reminds us of that approaching season of adolescence in which hopes are remembered,

fears deeply impressed, instruction gained,
and responsibilities incurred. The Apostle
John, adorned with every youthful grace, virtue's own image; the intrepid confidence of
confirmed manhood, vigilant of all things; the
mature age and reflective dignity of St. Peter,
whose whole appearance discloses that expressive wisdom, experience, and subdued passion,
which constitute the bulwark of social order
and improvement; and the decrepitude of
declining years, in which period magnified
reminiscenses and the value of the present
moment overpower the dissolving vision of
life's remaining term, finish the exhibition of
this part of the human scene. In another
view, our attention is drawn to its various
conditions of adversity and prosperity, its
vices and virtues, its derangements, its health,
its extremes of coarseness and refined beauty.

Raphael also intended, by an arrangement
of composition natural as picturesque, to des-
ignate the relative character of the two great

dispensations of the former and present world, both being included in his subject. In this endeavor he has equally succeeded in suggesting the sacred obligations and authority of the Mosaic Law, flowing from the sublime source of Deity, and perpetuated through prophets, priests, and kings, accompanied with all the pomp and circumstance of ceremonies, of fasts, and festivals, and commemorations calculated to command the mind of man and secure his obedience, and in displaying the initiatory progress and gentler spirit of Christianity; which, proceeding from the same Divine origin, is seen, in representation and in prospect, triumphing by its more perfect adaptation to human wants, its amelioration of religious and moral institutions, and its infinitely clearer elucidation of future "life and immortality."

The veil of ages seems to unfold as reflection looks back upon the scene. On the marble floor of the temple at Jerusalem stood

the Apostles, who, taught by the prediction
of one, greater than they, to know its fall,
even there laid the foundation of a new super-
structure; and as the former faded away, in
their prophetic view they beheld, rising in its
place, a building not made with hands, eternal, immutable,—the Temple of the Christian
Universe!

Thus, after an examination pursued with
close attention, spontaneously led on from excellence to excellence, we leave the contemplation of this picture, entirely convinced of
its claims on our regard, and with ideas suitable to the subject. Elevated and solemnized
by its higher import, the mind is also impressed with complacency and satisfaction, in
a subordinate view, at that dignity and beauty
of the human race which are ordained by
Providence, in the prescribed plan of nature,
to be the permanent order of its condition.
It perceives that disease, deformity, and dis-
tortion, although frequent, are departures

from the rule: it is reminded that prudential care and virtue, which administer to health and strength, are the preservatives of the former, and that neglect and vice are commonly the origin of the latter. The moral aim of the design, next in importance to its scriptural purpose, is to inculcate the sentiment of unfailing pity for human suffering, from whatever cause it may arise, and to animate the practice of that benevolence which, apart from the direct interposition of heavenly aid, is its proper antidote.

From beyond "that bourne from which no traveler returns," in solitude's dark hour, and through the still atmosphere of hallowed thought, a voice is heard; it swells upon the mental ear; it is the spirit of sacred hope that chants the hymn of praise and promise, "here, in eternal light and felicity issuing from the smile of Paternal Deity, the afflicted-weary are at rest, and the good receive their final recompense!"

Breinigsville, PA USA
14 July 2010
241795BV00003B/23/P